At the Skate Park

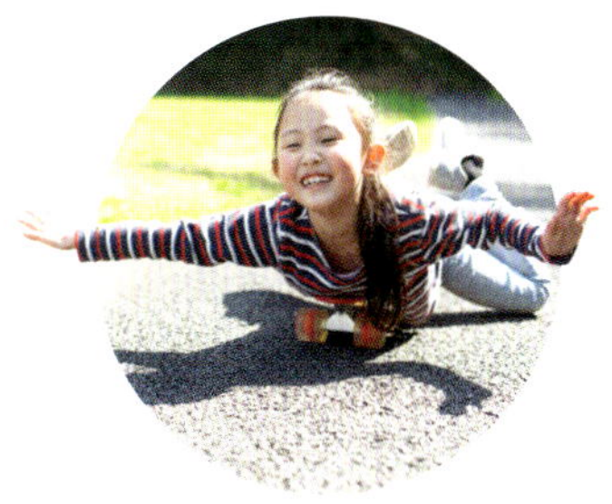

Written by
Stephen Rickard

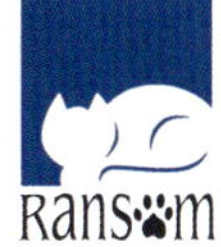

Ransom

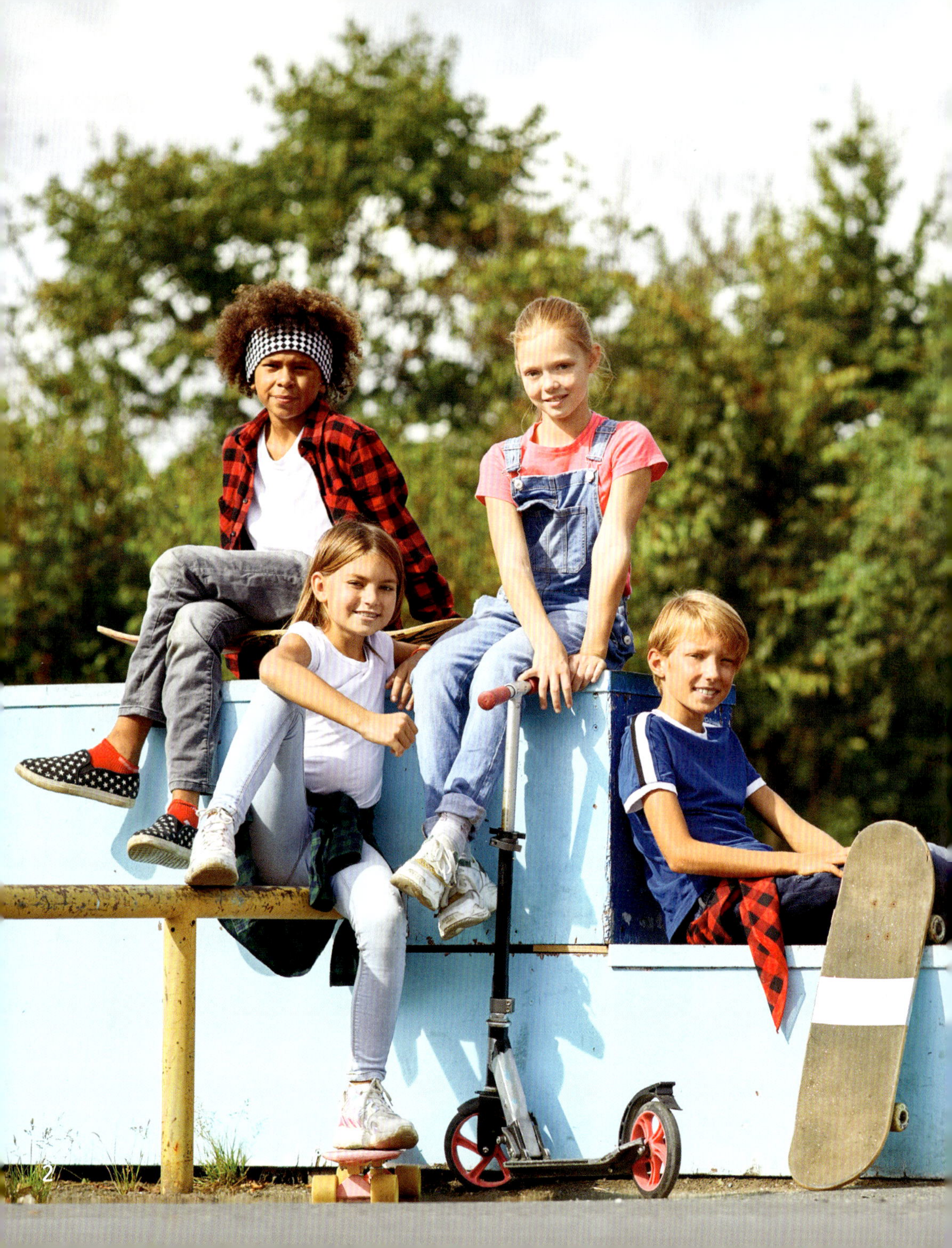

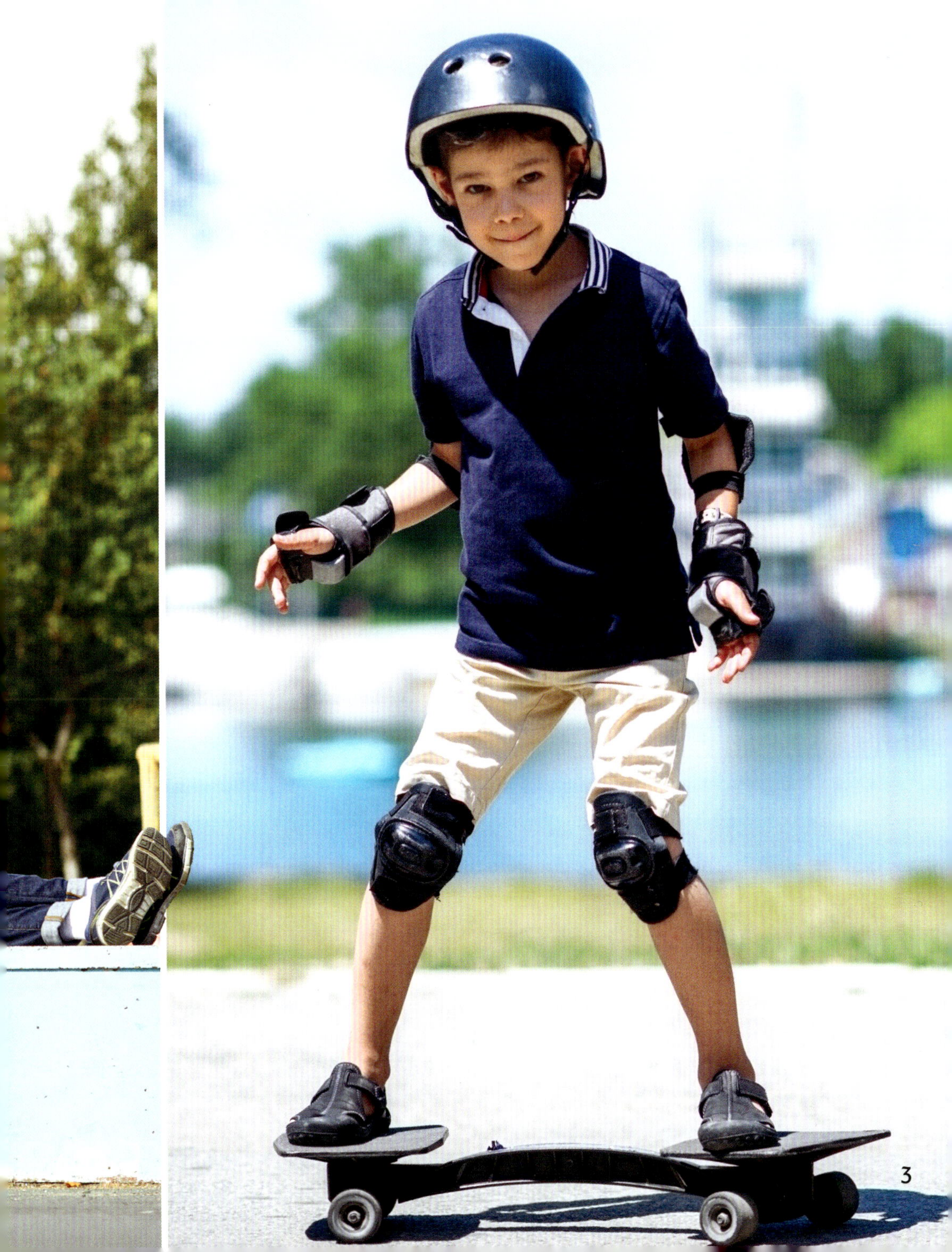

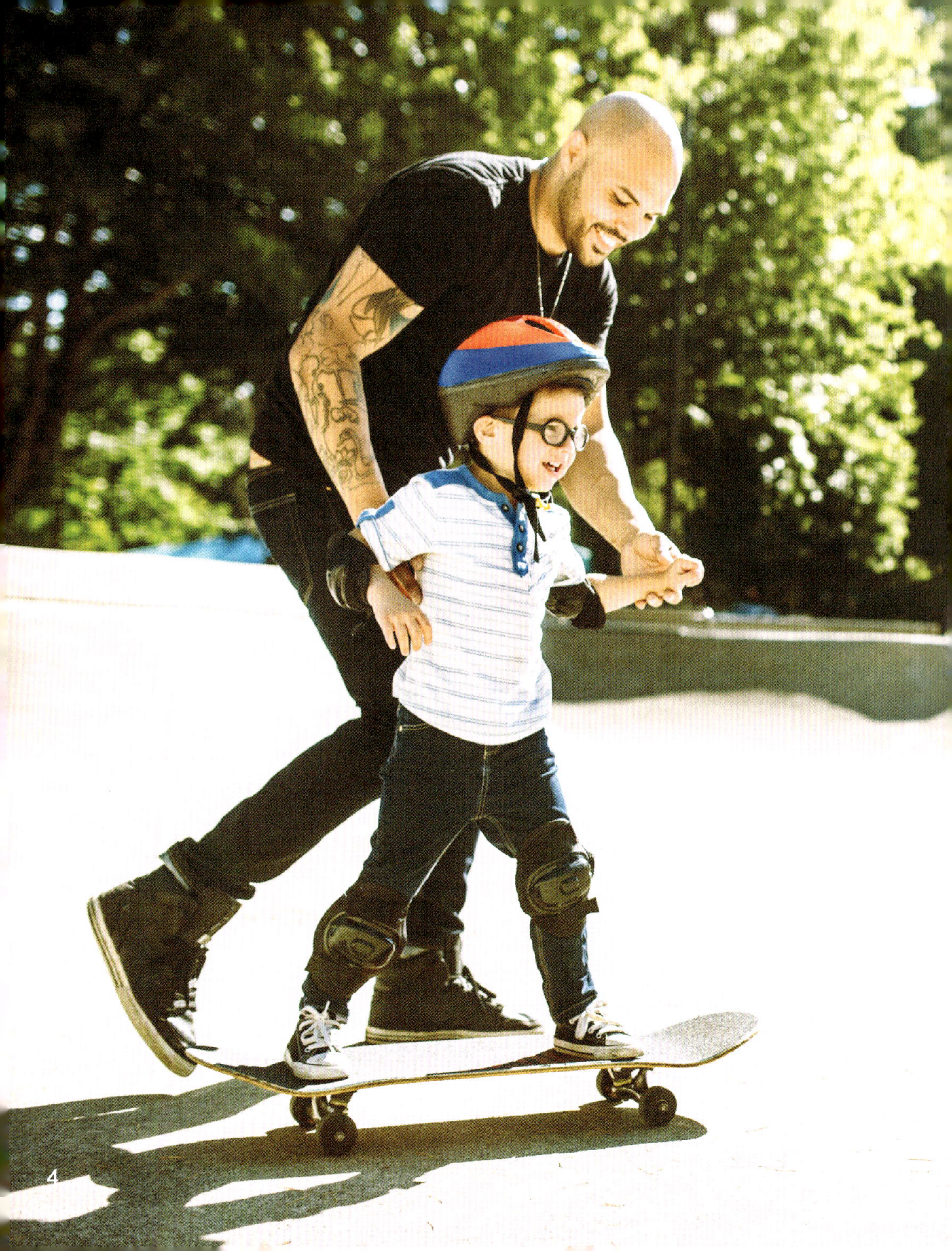

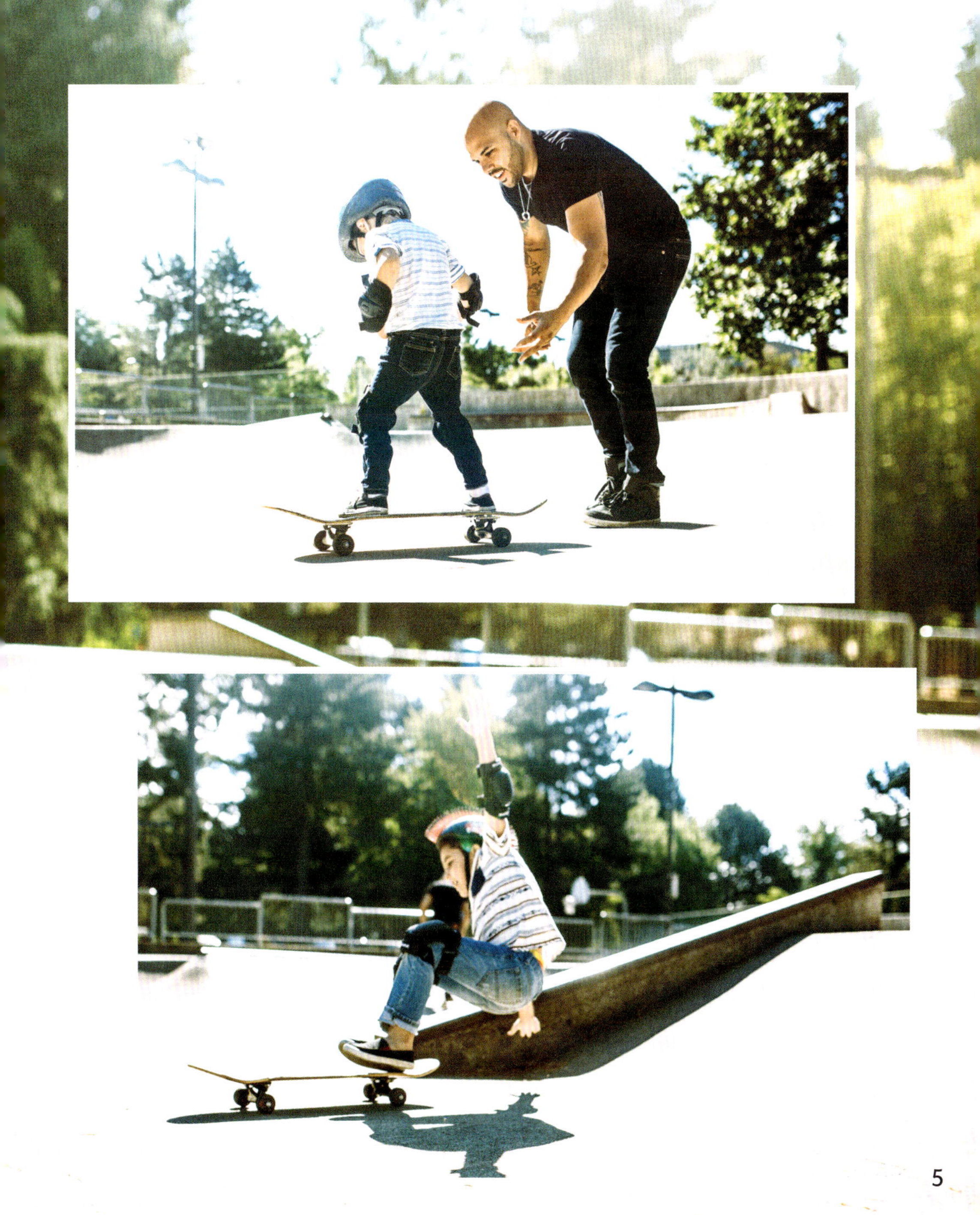

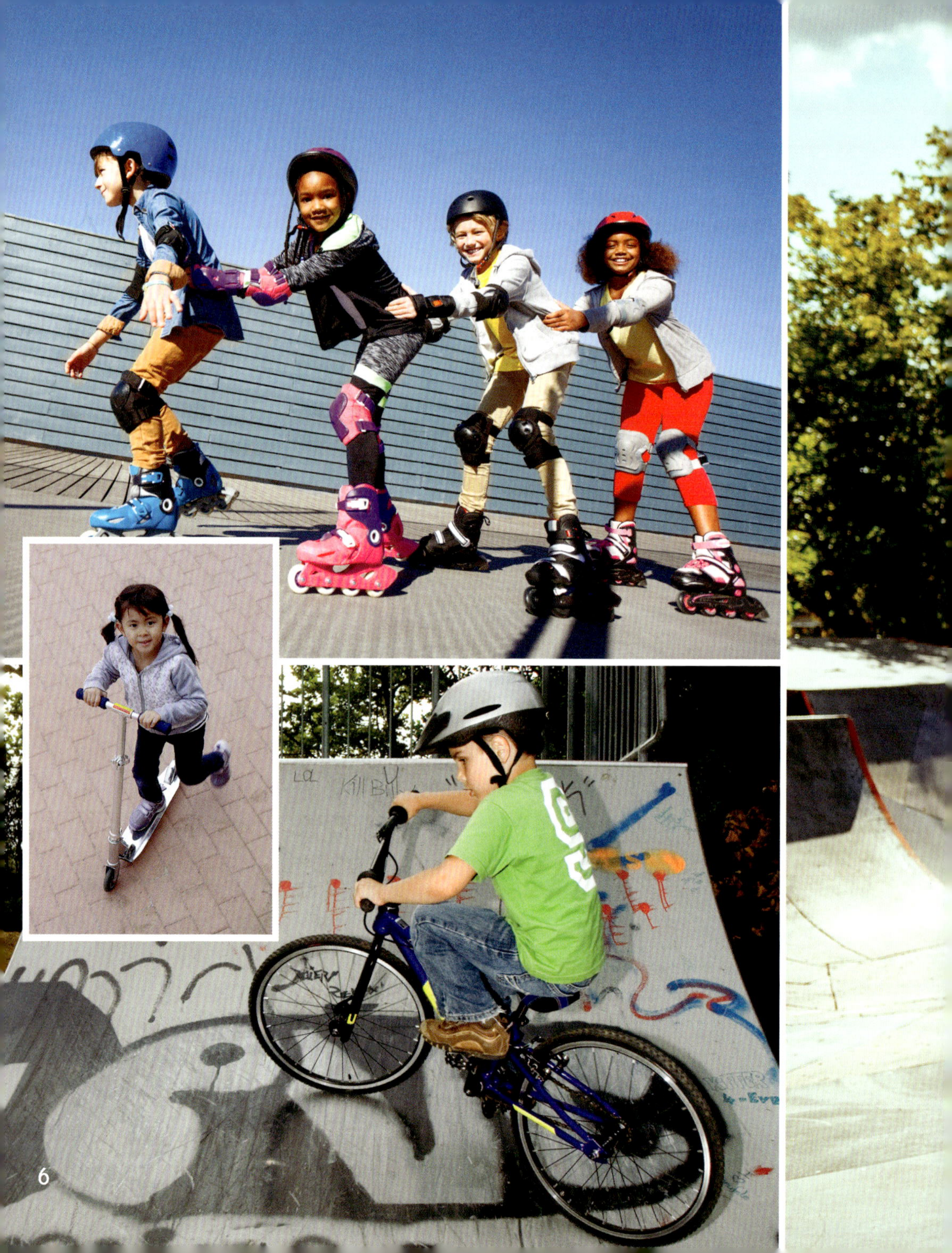

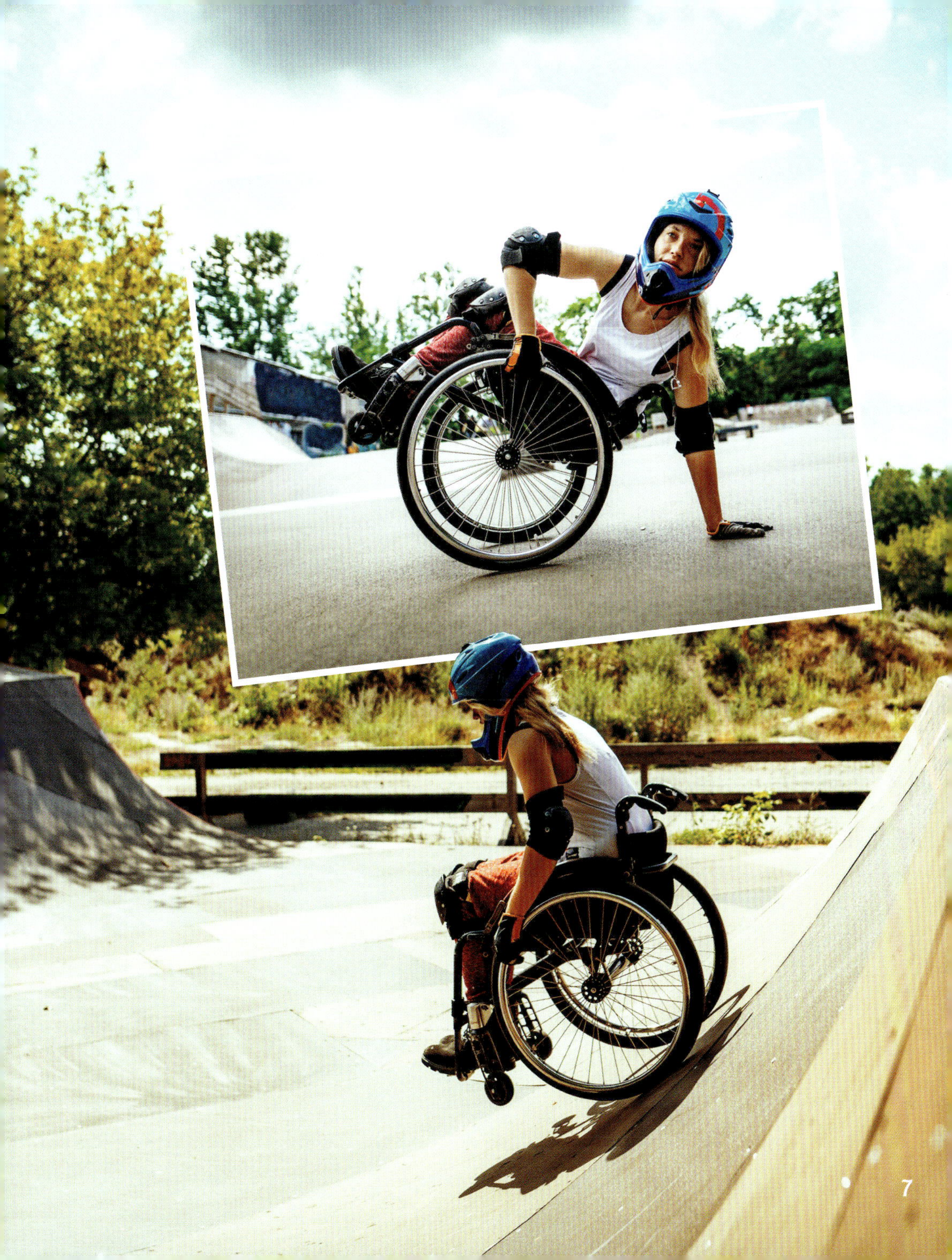

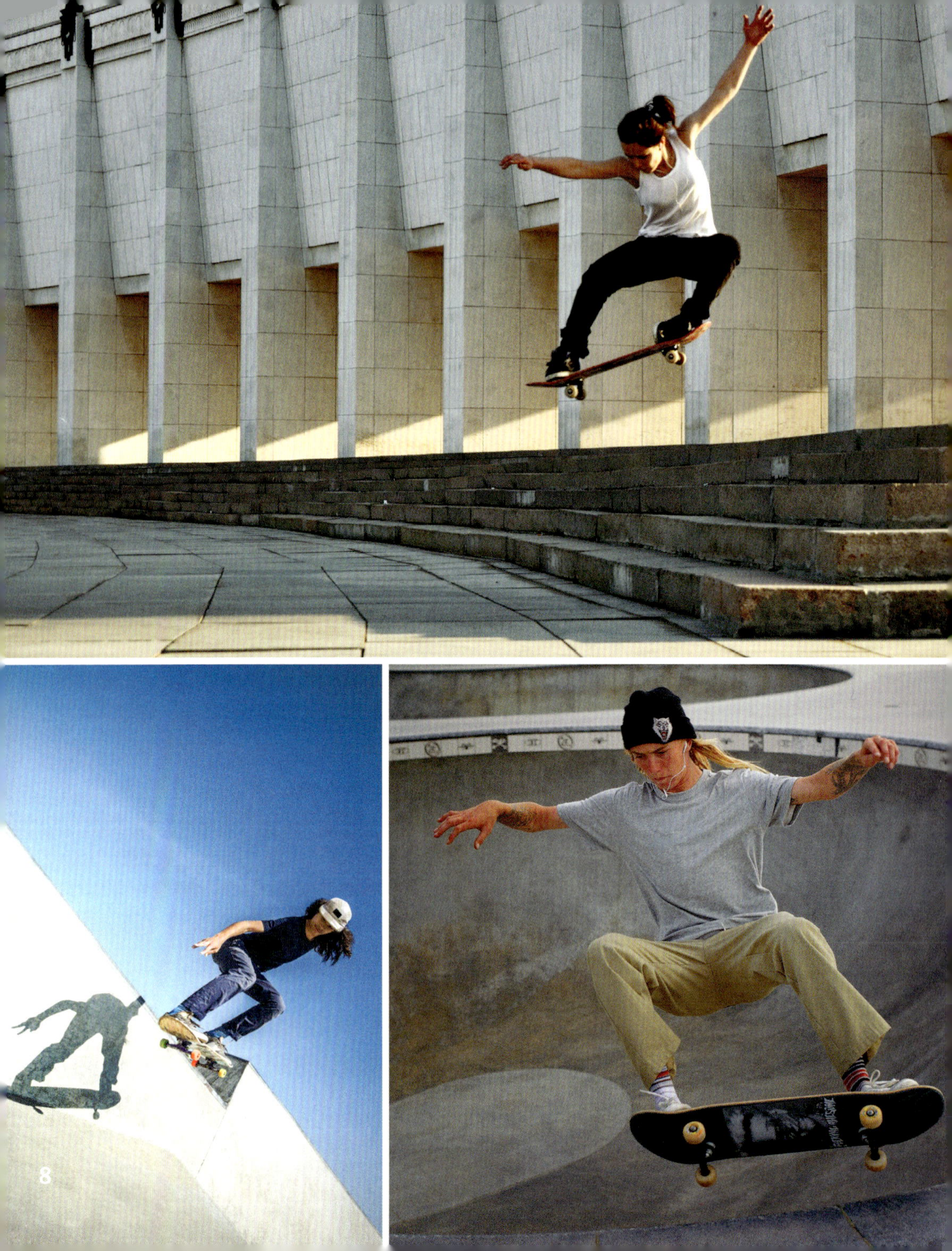